Spiders
and how they hunt

Jason Amber

Acknowledgements

Photos
Michael Leach / Oxford Scientific Films, page 6. J.A.L. Cooke / Oxford Scientific Films, page 7 top left and bottom left and page 24. Martin Wendler / NHPA, page 7 top right. Pascal Goetgheluck / Ardea London Ltd, page 7 bottom right and page 10. Hans Christoph Kappel / BBC Natural History Unit, page 8. Bob Fredrick / Oxford Scientific Films, page 12. David M. Dennis / Oxford Scientific Films, page 14. Stephen Dalton / NHPA, page 16. Garden Matters, page 18. Mantis Wildlife Films / Oxford Scientific Films, page 20. A.N.T. / NHPA, page 22.

Illustrations
All illustrations by Alan Male, Linden Artists

Heinemann Educational Publishers
Halley Court, Jordan Hill, Oxford OX2 8EJ
a division of Reed Educational & Professional Publishing Limited
www.heinemann.co.uk

Heinemann is a registered trademark of Reed Educational & Professional
Publishing Limited

First published 2000
Original edition © Reed Educational and Professional Publishing Ltd, 1999
Literary Satellites edition © Reed Educational and Professional Publishing Limited, 2000
Additional writing for Satellites edition by Christine Butterworth

04
10 9 8 7 6 5 4 3

ISBN 0 435 11987 7   *Spiders (and how they hunt)* single copy
ISBN 0 435 11991 5   *Spiders (and how they hunt)* 6 copy pack

Designed by M2
Printed and bound in Scotland by Scotprint

Also available at Stage 4 Literacy World Satellites
ISBN 0 435 11986 9   *LW Satellites: Alan Shearer: A Biography* single copy
ISBN 0 435 11990 7   *LW Satellites: Alan Shearer: A Biography* 6 copy pack

ISBN 0 435 11988 5   *LW Satellites: Big Issues* single copy
ISBN 0 435 11992 3   *LW Satellites: Big Issues* 6 copy pack

ISBN 0 435 11989 3   *LW Satellites: Quakes, Floods and Other Disasters* single copy
ISBN 0 435 11993 1   *LW Satellites: Quakes, Floods and Other Disasters* 6 copy pack

ISBN 0 435 11995 8   *LW Satellites: Teachers' Guide Stage 4*
ISBN 0 435 11994 X   *LW Satellites: Guided Reading Cards Stage 4*

Contents

Key

The symbols below are used in this book to show the habitats of the different spiders.

Desert

Grasslands

Woodland

Gardens

Ponds and lakes

Introduction

There are 30,000 different types or 'species' of spider. They can be found all over the world – from hot, dry deserts to cool, wet rainforests. One can even live underwater. There are no spiders in the Arctic, the Antarctic and deep oceans. All spiders eat other animals, they are carnivores, but they hunt in different ways.

Arachnids

Spider are not insects. They are animals called arachnids (say *araknids*).

Insects, such as ants, bees and beetles, have six legs.

Arachnids, such as spiders and scorpions, have eight legs.

	Insects	Arachnids
Legs	6	8
Antennae (say *anteneye*)	2	none
Wings	most have 2 or 4	none
Has a poisonous bite or sting	some	nearly all
Eats plants	some	none
Eats other animals	some	all

4

Parts of a spider

All spiders have:
- eight legs
- large jaws and sharp fangs to bite prey
- spinnerets to spin the silk to make webs

Most spiders have:
- eight eyes, but many cannot see well
- hairs on their legs to sense other animals coming near
- fangs they use to inject poison into their prey.

Some spiders have:
- six, four or two eyes
- no eyes at all – they live in dark caves and do not need to see

claw

eyes

fangs

hairs

jaw

abdomen

spinnerets

leg

head and thorax

All arachnids have a body in two parts: head and thorax, and abdomen.

5

Catching prey

Spiders catch their prey in different ways. Some lie in wait until their prey is near, then jump out. Some hunt for their prey, and others weave their silk into a trap. Most spiders inject poison into their prey to kill or paralyse it. Then they eat it.

Don't kill spiders!

A few spiders found in hot countries are a danger to people. They only bite to protect themselves. Most spiders cannot bite and are harmless. They also eat insects that spread diseases, such as flies and cockroaches.

Many spiders weave webs of silk to trap their prey.

Eyes, jaws and legs

Spiders that hunt for prey need to see well. Many have large eyes.

Spiders that lie in wait, or trap their prey in webs, do not need to see well. Many have small, weak eyes.

Jumping spider

Orb web spider

Crab spider

Spiders that grab hold of their prey to bite it have strong legs.

Purse web spider

Spiders that stab their prey to hold it often have huge fangs.

Habitat	Size	Latin family name
	13–40mm	Ctenizidae

Ambush spiders

Trapdoor spiders

These large spiders use their strong jaws to dig out soil and make a burrow. They line it with silk, and make a door from soil and silk. Then they hide inside, waiting for prey.

Trapdoor spiders ambush their prey at night.

Catching prey

1 Some trapdoor spiders spin 'trip wires' of silk by the trap door. The spider hides inside the trap.

2 The trapdoor spider keeps its legs on the silk trip wires. When it feels an insect touch the trip wires, it rushes out. It grabs the prey with its huge jaws, injecting poison.

3 The insect is paralysed, and the spider pulls it down into the trap.

9

Habitat	Size	Latin family name
	12–17mm	Atypidae

Ambush spiders

Purse web spiders

Purse web spiders also dig burrows, like trapdoor spiders (see page 8).
They weave a tube of silk. They lay this outside the burrow, hidden
under a layer of soil. The spider hides inside the tube, waiting for its prey.

Purse web spiders have huge fangs.

Catching prey

1 The purse web spider waits, hidden in the tube. When an insect lands on the tube, it makes the tube shake.

2 When the spider feels the tube shake, it runs under the insect and stabs its huge fangs into the insect's belly.

3 Then it drags the insect down the tube and into its burrow to eat.

Habitat	Size	Latin family name
	4–15mm	Thomisidae

Ambush spiders

Crab spiders

These flat, round spiders have big front legs and walk sideways, like crabs do. They sit on flowers or under stones, waiting for their prey. A crab spider may even attack a big bumblebee.

Crab spiders are camouflaged so they are hard to spot.

Catching prey

1 The crab spider waits on a flower. Its colour helps to hide it, and it can keep still all day if it has to.

2 When an insect lands on the flower, the spider moves so slowly that the insect does not notice.

3 The spider's back legs hang on to the flower while its big front legs grab the insect. Its fangs bite the insect, injecting it with poison. Then it sucks out the insect's insides.

13

Habitat	Size	Latin family name
	4–34mm	Lycosidae

Hunters

Wolf spiders

These large spiders can run fast on their long legs. Their large eyes help them see well. Some wolf spiders live by ponds and chase insects across the water.

Wolf spiders always hunt alone.

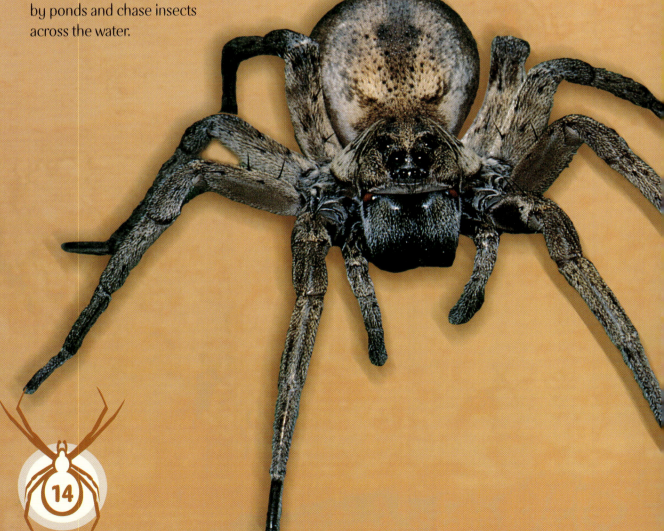

14

Catching prey

1 The wolf spider runs along the ground, looking for prey.

2 When the spider sees its prey, it stands still. Then it creeps forward, like a cat stalking a mouse.

3 Suddenly it dashes at the prey and bites it. The poison paralyses the insect, and the spider eats it.

Habitat	Size	Latin family name
	4–15mm	Salticidae

Hunters

Jumping spiders

These small spiders have short, strong legs and big eyes. They can jump a very long way: up to 40 times the length of their body! They can see better than all other spiders. Some can leap up and catch flying insects.

Jumping spiders can walk up glass and not fall off because they have tiny hooks on their feet.

Catching prey

1 The jumping spider runs along the ground, or up walls or trees, looking for prey. Once the spider sees it, it stalks its prey slowly.

2 Suddenly the spider jumps at the insect. As it falls, it spins a 'life-line' of silk behind it. If the spider misses the prey, it pulls itself back up its silk line.

3 If it catches the prey, it injects it with poison.

Habitat	Size	Latin family name
	3–45mm	Araneidae

Orb web spiders

Orb web spiders spin large webs from sticky silk threads. Flying insects get stuck in the web, day and night, and the spider eats them all. However, if a stinging insect, like a wasp, gets trapped in the web, the spider may cut it free.

The orb web spider's strong web is hard to see.

18

Catching prey

1 The orb web spider has poor sight, so it has to sense its prey using hairs on its legs and feet. It waits on the web, or hides nearby in a silk lair. Its feet touch the long 'signal' threads that lead from the web.

2 When an insect flies into the web, it struggles. This makes the 'signal' threads shake. The spider feels the shaking with its feet. It can even tell how big the insect is.

3 The spider rushes out and bites the prey to paralyse it. Then it wraps it in silk and takes it off to eat in its lair or in the web.

19

Habitat	Size	Latin family name
	10–18mm	Dinopidae

Net-throwers

Net-throwing spiders are nocturnal. They weave a small, stretchy net of silk which they hold in their front legs. They drop it over passing insects or hold it up to trap moths flying by.

The net-throwing spider hunts at night. By day, the net hangs on a leaf, ready for the spider to use at night.

Catching prey

1 The net-throwing spider hangs, head down, just above the ground. It holds its net, waiting for an insect to pass.

2 When its prey arrives, the spider stretches the net to make it bigger.

3 The spider pushes the sticky net down over the insect. It wraps it up and bites it so it cannot move.

Habitat	Size	Latin family name
	5–18mm	Mastophora

Bolas spiders

These small, fat spiders spend the day hiding under leaves. At night they spin a silk thread with a large, sticky droplet on the end. They use this thread (or 'bolas') to catch prey.

This spider swings its bolas.

22

Catching prey

1 The bolas spider hangs from one silk thread. It spins another for its bolas.

2 When a moth flies near, the spider begins to swing the bolas.

3 When the moth is near, the spider swings the bolas out. The moth sticks to the droplet. The spider pulls the moth in and bites it.

Habitat	Size	Latin family name
	15mm	Argyroneta

Water spiders

These small spiders are the only ones that hunt underwater. They weave their webs among the weeds. Then they drag air bubbles under the water and trap them in the threads of the web. The spiders live inside the air bubble, like a diver.

The spider traps air bubbles in its nest.

Catching prey

1 The spider waits for prey, breathing the air in its bubble.

2 The spider has very fine hairs on its legs. These can sense an insect moving near its nest.

3 The spider rushes out of the bubble and bites the prey to inject it with poison. It drags the prey into its nest to eat.

How can you tell spiders apart?

This Venn diagram sorts different spiders into groups.

FAST RUNNER

Wolf spider

Jumping spider

WAITS ON FLOWER FOR PREY

Crab spider

SPINS SILK TO CATCH PREY

Bolas spider

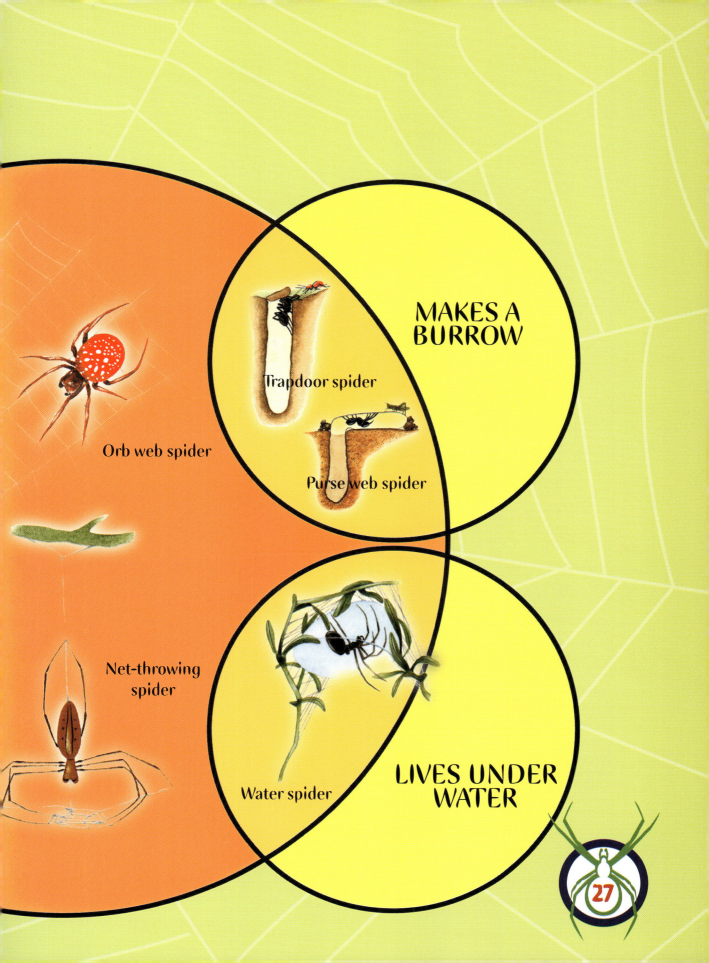

MAKES A
BURROW

Trapdoor spider

Purse web spider

Orb web spider

Net-throwing
spider

Water spider

LIVES UNDER
WATER

27

How spiders hunt

This flow chart describes the different ways spiders hunt.

Spins silk to catch prey	→	Makes a burrow	→
	→	Makes a web to live by or in	→
	→	Throws web or swings silk at prey	→
Does not use silk to catch prey	→	Good eyesight	→
	→	Poor eyesight	→

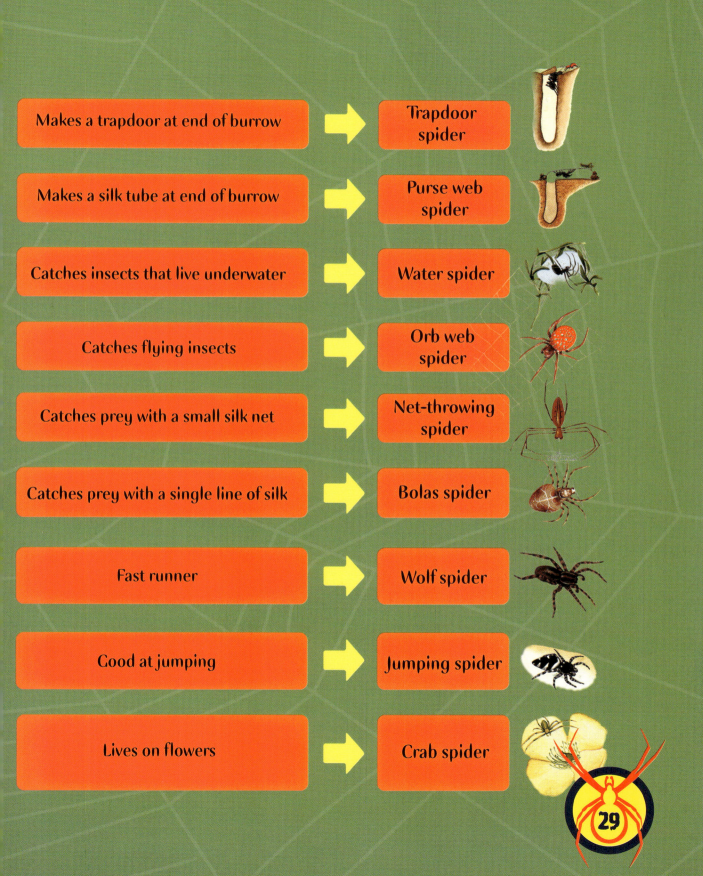

Makes a trapdoor at end of burrow	➡	Trapdoor spider
Makes a silk tube at end of burrow	➡	Purse web spider
Catches insects that live underwater	➡	Water spider
Catches flying insects	➡	Orb web spider
Catches prey with a small silk net	➡	Net-throwing spider
Catches prey with a single line of silk	➡	Bolas spider
Fast runner	➡	Wolf spider
Good at jumping	➡	Jumping spider
Lives on flowers	➡	Crab spider

Glossary

abdomen
the rear part of an arachnid's or insect's body

ambush
surprise attack from a hidden position

antennae
two tubes on an insect's head, used to smell, feel or hear

camouflage
to blend in with surroundings

carnivores
animals that eat other animals

lair
burrow, nest or home

nocturnal
active during the night

paralysed
unable to move

prey
an animal that is hunted by another for food

silk
very thin but strong thread produced by spiders and some insects

species
a group of living things that are very similar

thorax
the middle part of an arachnid's or insect's body

Bibliography

Harlow, Rosie and Morgan, Gareth, *Minibeasts*,
Fun with Science, Kingfisher, 1991

Hillyard, Paul, *Spiders Photoguide*, Collins Gem,
HarperCollins Publishers, 1997

Kalman, Bobbie, *Web Weavers and Other Spiders,*
Crabtree Publishing Co, 1997

Parsons, Alexandra, *Amazing Spiders*,
Eyewitness Juniors, Dorling Kindersley, 1990

Preston-Mafham, Ken, *Spiders—The illustrated identifier to over 90 species*,
The Apple Press, 1998

Preston-Mafham, Rod and Ken, *Spiders of the World*,
Blandford Press, 1989

Preston-Mafham, Rod and Ken, *The Natural History of Spiders*,
Crowood Press, 1996

Preston-Mafham, Rod, *Spiders, an illustrated guide*,
Blandford Press, 1991

Theodorou, Rod and Telford, Carole, *Spider and Scorpion*,
Spot the Difference, Heinemann Library, 1997

Watts, Barrie, *Spider's Web*,
Stopwatch Books, A & C Black, 1990

Index